Collins

Cherry Blossoms

General Awareness Workbook

UKG

FS3

SERIES EDITOR: RANI THIPPAVAZZULA

AF655596

Preface

Cherry Blossoms provides graded, age-appropriate learning opportunities targeting holistic skill development for children in the age group of 3 years to 8 years. The series aligns with the vision outlined in the National Education Policy, 2020 for early years. It spreads across five levels, Nursery (Foundational Stage 1) to Class 2 (Foundational Stage 5). The books use a combination of hands-on activities, frequent recapitulation and child-friendly artwork to facilitate learning.

The series comprises **40 books** and spans **English**, **Maths**, **General Awareness**, and **Art and Craft**. The series comes bundled with a **workbook** for each subject and a book of **rhymes** and **stories** for Foundational Stage 1 to 3.

This series integrates the essence of **NIPUN Bharat** guidelines, which extensively deal with Foundational Literacy and Numeracy. The series aims to motivate learners to read independently, to improve their vocabulary, number sense and spatial understanding. The **Foundational Literacy and Numeracy (FLN)** skills include the skills for developing their critical thinking, logical reasoning and creative skills, as well as the skills to enhance their ability to express themselves both verbally and in writing.

Cherry Blossoms Teacher Support Materials include:

Teacher's Resource Books: Comprises stories, activity banks, classroom management and assessment guidelines

Multimedia eBook: Consists of animations, audio, video, slide shows, and interactive exercises

Print-ready Worksheets: Additional worksheets for practice and reinforcement, present in the digital support

Digital Flashcards: Flashcards with embedded sounds and animations for letter formation and letter-sound association

Animations and Songs: Animated stories and rhymes set to tune

Interactive Games: Interactivities to reinforce concepts in a fun and engaging manner

A note on the activity banks (included in the Teacher's Manuals)

The activity banks comprise hands-on activities that will help children develop the requisite skills to attain age-appropriate learning goals. In keeping with Howard Gardener's theory of multiple intelligences, the activity banks include options and variations that enable teachers to provide a planned cycle of experiences and opportunities, which foster each type of intelligence, to every child in their classrooms. The activity banks equip teachers to use the strengths of children as a means of complementing their less developed areas by valuing and nurturing the inherent abilities of the children.

Rani Thippavazzula, former Academic Director, Ravindra Bharathi Group is an eminent educationist with over two decades of experience in teaching, administration and curriculum design and development. As an Academic Advisor for chain schools pan India, she is proficient in developing learning products and is a specialist in Differentiated Instruction, Enterprise Education and Early Childhood Education.

Learning and Development During the Early Years

The early years are the most significant years for growth, development and learning. During this period, children need adequate opportunities for stimulating experiences as these favourably affect various learning abilities. Learning experiences, when chosen and planned properly, fuel the innate curiosity of children, and stimulate their thought processes.

The goal of learning during the early years is to enhance the all-round development of personality and to inculcate healthy attitudes, life skills and good values. Creative play, well thought-out games and developmentally appropriate activities help children develop the necessary skills to achieve these goals. The skills that children need to acquire can broadly be categorized as:

Motor:
Motor skills pertain not only to gross motor activities like walking and jumping but also include fine motor activities like the ability to hold a pencil and write. The development of motor skills is facilitated through several graded activities.

Personal, Social and Emotional:
Personal, social and emotional development, necessary for the overall personality development of children, is achieved using a combination of hands-on activities, role plays and thought-provoking stories and rhymes.

Linguistic:
The ability to listen, speak, read and write is critical to success in formal learning environments.

Mathematical:
The development of mathematical ideas and concepts is important at this stage since children will continue to build on this learning for most of their years of schooling.

Knowledge and Understanding of the World:
This is achieved through activities that enable children to explore their surroundings at home and in the school, and interact with the people that they see around them.

Health and Safety: The idea of health and safety is introduced through activities, stories and retelling of real-life experiences to encourage children to focus on health and well-being.

Creative:
Creative skills are developed through a host of activities involving art, craft, painting, roleplays, etc.

Logical and Rational Thinking:
Activities that involve simple puzzles, pattern-completion and visual discrimination help children to develop logical and rational thinking skills.

Contents

Community Helpers

Match the following.

 • doctor • 

 • tailor • 

 • postman • 

• teacher • 

 • grocer • 

 • cobbler • 

Colours

Colour the pictures with your favourite colour.

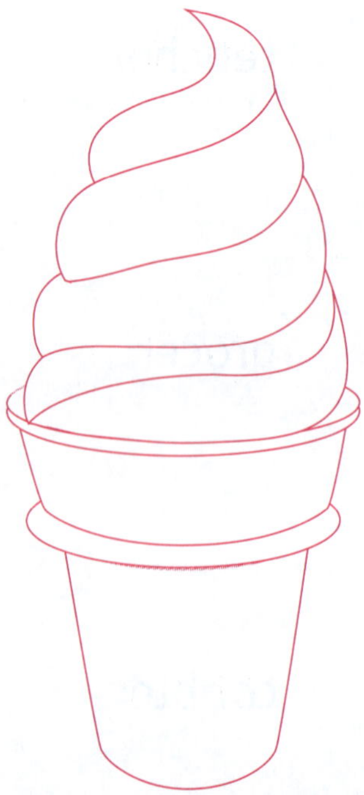

Fruits

Draw and colour your favourite fruit.

Look at the fruits and talk about them. Which one do you eat?

apple

banana

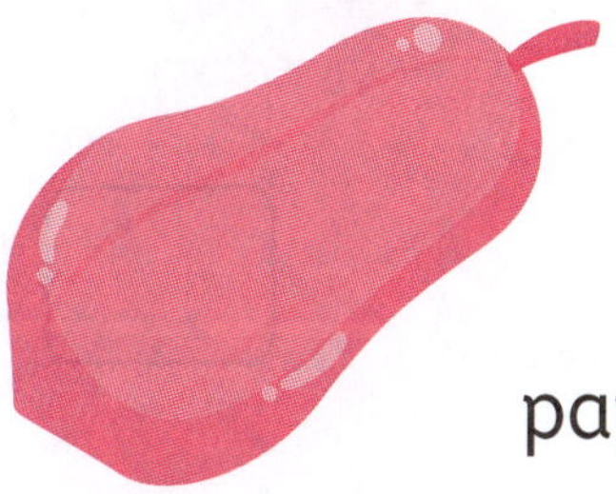

papaya

mango

Vegetables

Tick (✓) the vegetables you know.

okra ☐

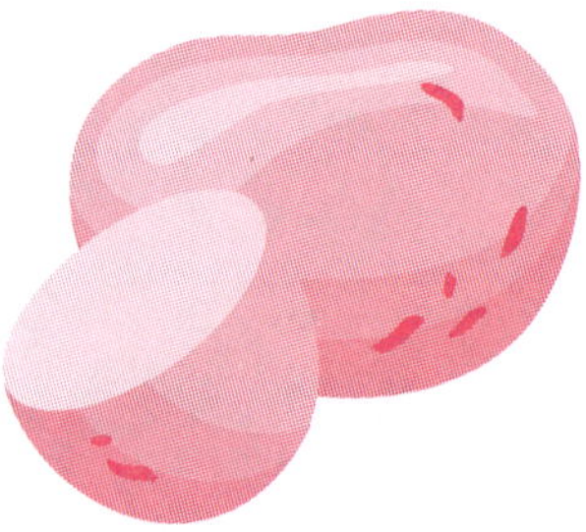

potato ☐

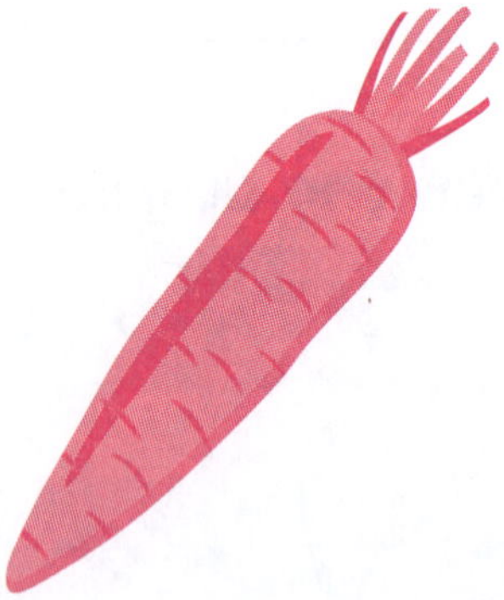

carrot ☐

cauliflower ☐

Safety

Read the safety measures. Tick (✓) the ones you follow.

I do not touch electrical appliances. ☐

I do not touch hot things. ☐

I do not jump on the bed. ☐

I do not play with sharp objects. ☐

I do not open the door for any stranger. ☐

I do not run on the stairs. ☐

I do not push anybody. ☐

I do not shout. ☐

I always walk with elders. ☐

I never cross the road alone. ☐

Seasons

Match the following.

rainy season

winter season

spring season

summer season

Clothes We Wear

Match the following.

 • • winter

 • • summer

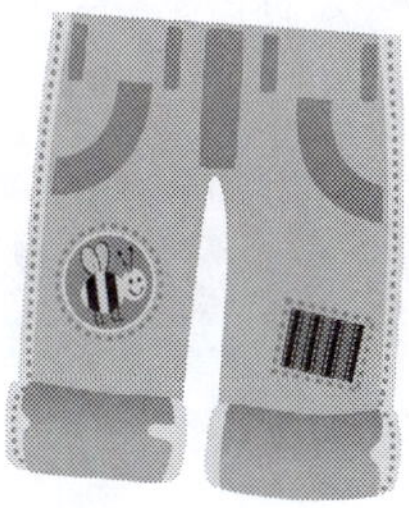 • • rainy season

Draw a sweater  and a skirt  in the correct box.

summer	winter

Animals on the Farm

Look at the animals on the farm.

Draw one animal that you like from the farm.

Animal in the Zoo

Look at these animals. Cross out (✗) the animals you see in a zoo.

Draw your favourite animal from the zoo.

Animals in Water

Read the names of these animals. Talk about them.

fish

octopus

whale

dolphin

Do you have fish at home?

Yes ☐ No ☐

Animals at Home

Draw a picture of your pet animal.

Tick (✓) the pet animal you like.

Birds Around Us

Look at the birds. Talk about them. Tick (✓) the ones you see daily.

☐

parrot

☐

pigeon

☐

sparrow

☐

swan

☐

crow

☐

hen

Young Ones of Animals

Match the animals with their young ones.

Insects

Tick (✓) the insects you see around you.

butterfly ☐

bee ☐

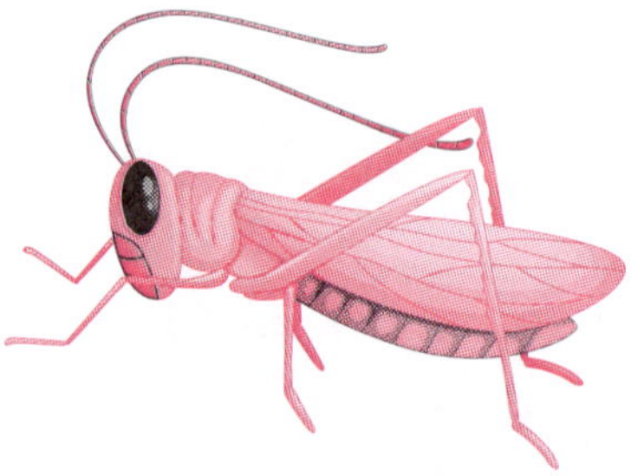

grasshopper ☐

mosquito ☐

ant ☐

Gadgets at Home

Tick (✓) the gadgets you have at home.

Draw a fan and a mobile in the given box.

Means of Transport

Match the following.

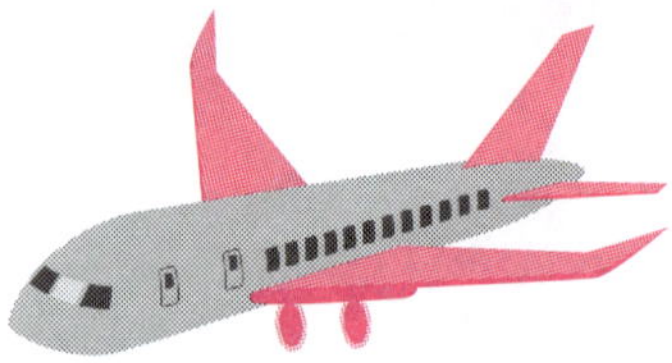

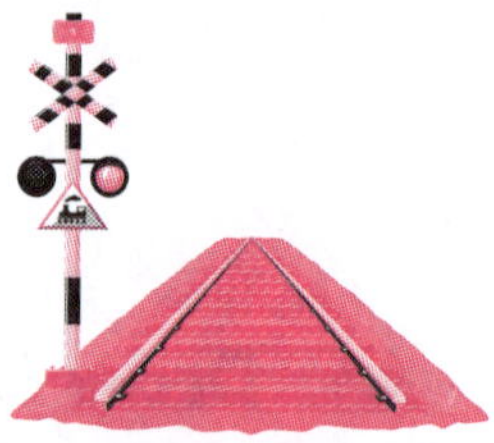

Paste picture of the means of transport in the correct box.

air transport	water transport

Months of the Year

Read the months of the year.

January February

March April May

June July August

September October

November December

Trace and write the names of the months.

January February

March April

May June

July August

September October

November December

Fun time!

Draw and colour anything you like that you see around you.